The Quiet Side of Wealth

G.P. Upadhyay

Published by GYAN PRAKASH UPADHYAY, 2026.

THE QUIET SIDE OF WEALTH

First edition. January 5, 2026.

ISBN: 979-8233046605

Written by G.P. Upadhyay.

Table of Contents

To those who choose patience over noise,calm over comparison,and long-term thinking in a short-term world.

"Wealth grows quietly when behavior stays calm long enough for time to matter."

G.P. Upadhyay

Chapter 1: Money Is Not a Math Problem

Most people believe money is about intelligence.

They think those who succeed financially are smarter, faster, or better at numbers. They assume wealth is built by people who understand spreadsheets, markets, or complex strategies. This belief is comforting. It suggests that if money is just math, then success is predictable and fair.

But real life quietly proves something else.

Some of the smartest people struggle with money for decades. At the same time, people with average intelligence—and sometimes very little formal education—build lasting wealth. This contradiction exists everywhere, across countries, cultures, and generations.

The reason is simple.

Money is not primarily a math problem.

It is a behavior problem.

When we make money decisions, we rarely behave like calculators. We behave like humans. Humans are emotional, biased, impatient, fearful, hopeful, and deeply influenced by their past.

Two people can receive the same financial advice and experience completely different outcomes—not because the advice was wrong, but because their behavior was different.

One person stays calm during uncertainty.

The other panics.

One person waits patiently.

The other demands fast results.

One person avoids unnecessary risk.

The other feels overconfident.

The numbers didn't change. The behavior did.

Think about the biggest financial decisions people make in life: saving, investing, spending, borrowing, or starting a business. Very few of these decisions happen in a quiet, emotionless environment.

They happen during moments of stress.

During excitement.

During fear of missing out.

During pressure to look successful.

In those moments, intelligence takes a back seat. Behavior takes control.

Consider two investors with the same income and the same opportunities.

One stays invested during difficult times. The other exits at the first sign of discomfort. Over decades, the difference in outcomes becomes enormous.

Not because one understood money better.

But because one understood themselves better.

We like to believe that financial mistakes come from lack of knowledge. In reality, most mistakes come from perfectly normal human reactions.

Fear makes people sell too early.

Ego makes people take unnecessary risks.

Impatience makes people chase shortcuts.

Comparison makes people overspend.

These behaviors are not rare. They are universal.

That is why money advice that sounds perfect on paper often fails in real life. It ignores the emotional side of decision-making.

There is another reason behavior matters more than intelligence: time.

Wealth is rarely built in dramatic moments. It grows quietly, slowly, and often invisibly. Small decisions repeated consistently over long periods matter far more than bold, intelligent moves made occasionally.

Patience compounds.

Discipline compounds.

Calm thinking compounds.

These traits are not measured by IQ tests.

This book is not about how to outsmart the market, find secret strategies, or predict the future. Those approaches appeal to intelligence. They rarely lead to peace or consistency.

This book is about understanding why people behave the way they do with money—and how small changes in behavior can lead to dramatically better outcomes.

Not richer-looking lives.

But more stable ones.

More flexible ones.

More peaceful ones.

If there is one idea to remember from this chapter, it is this:

Financial success is not about being smarter than others.

It is about being calmer than your emotions when it matters most.

In the chapters ahead, we will explore how fear, confidence, time, luck, comparison, and patience quietly shape financial lives—often more than any formula ever could.

Money may involve numbers.

But wealth is built through behavior.

The most important financial skill is not intelligence.

It is emotional control over long periods of time.

Chapter 2: Everyone Has a Different Money Story

People often assume money decisions are universal.

They believe that if two people earn the same income, live in similar places, and face similar opportunities, they should make similar financial choices. When they don't, judgment follows. One person is called careless. The other is called conservative. One is praised for taking risks. The other is criticized for being too cautious.

But these judgments miss something important.

Everyone carries a different money story.

A money story is not written in textbooks.

It is written through experience.

It is shaped by childhood, family conversations, economic conditions, success, failure, fear, and luck. Long before people understand interest rates or investments, they absorb beliefs about money from what they see and feel.

Some people grow up watching money disappear quickly. Others grow up watching it accumulate slowly. Some see money as safety. Others see it as freedom. Some see it as fragile. Others see it as endless.

These experiences quietly guide decisions for decades.

Imagine two people who both lose money during a market downturn.

One has lived through financial instability before. They have seen income vanish, opportunities disappear, and recovery take years. For them, loss feels dangerous. Selling feels like protection.

The other has lived through growth, stability, and recovery. They have seen setbacks reversed over time. For them, loss feels temporary. Staying invested feels reasonable.

Both reactions are logical within their own stories.

Neither is stupid.

Neither is irrational.

They are responding to their past.

This is why money advice often fails.

Advice assumes a shared background.

Reality never provides one.

Telling someone to "take more risk" ignores the fear shaped by earlier losses. Telling someone to "be patient" ignores the anxiety formed by uncertainty. Even good advice can sound unrealistic when it conflicts with personal history.

People don't reject advice because they don't understand it.

They reject it because it doesn't fit their story.

Money stories also explain why comparison is so dangerous.

When you compare your financial progress to someone else's, you are comparing outcomes without comparing backgrounds. You see their success but not the risks they were comfortable taking. You see their lifestyle but not the safety net behind it.

Two people can make the same decision and experience very different consequences. One had room to fail. The other did not.

Without knowing someone's full story, comparison becomes misleading—and often expensive.

There is no such thing as a "normal" relationship with money.

Some people value security above all else.

Some value growth.

Some value flexibility.

Some value simplicity.

None of these priorities are wrong. Problems begin when people try to live according to someone else's money story.

That is when discomfort appears.

That is when stress grows.

That is when regret follows.

Understanding your own money story does not mean staying trapped in it.

It means recognizing it.

When you understand why certain financial decisions feel uncomfortable—or overly attractive—you gain clarity. You can separate fear from logic. You can question habits instead of blindly following them.

Self-awareness creates choice.

Without it, behavior runs on autopilot.

The most useful financial advice is not universal rules.

It is personal alignment.

A good financial plan is one you can stick to—not one that looks impressive. A sustainable approach matters more than an optimal one. The best strategy is the one that fits your temperament, your past, and your ability to remain calm when things go wrong.

If there is one lesson in this chapter, it is this:

Your financial decisions make sense when viewed through your personal history—even when they look irrational to others.

Wealth is not built by copying someone else's story.

It is built by understanding your own.

There is no single right way to handle money.

There is only the way that aligns with your experiences, values, and ability to stay consistent.

Chapter 3: Past Experiences Control Future Decisions

Most financial decisions feel like choices made in the present.

In reality, they are reactions to the past.

Long before people sit down to plan their finances, their minds are already shaped by what they have experienced. Wins create confidence. Losses create caution. Scarcity creates fear. Stability creates patience.

These forces operate quietly, often without awareness.

A single strong experience can outweigh years of information.

Someone who lived through a major loss may carry that memory forever. Even if the circumstances never repeat, the emotional imprint remains. Risk starts to feel dangerous, even when it is reasonable. Safety becomes the priority, even when it limits growth.

On the other hand, someone who experienced early success may develop confidence that feels permanent. Risk feels familiar. Setbacks feel temporary. This confidence can lead to bold decisions—sometimes wisely, sometimes dangerously.

Neither response is unusual.

Both are human.

Past experiences do not fade evenly.

Negative experiences tend to leave deeper marks than positive ones. Loss is remembered longer than gain. Fear lasts longer than excitement. This imbalance explains why people often avoid risk even when the odds are in their favor.

The brain is designed to protect, not to optimize.

From an evolutionary perspective, avoiding danger mattered more than maximizing opportunity. That instinct still influences modern financial behavior—even when the environment has changed.

This explains why people often repeat the same patterns.

Someone who experienced sudden loss may overvalue certainty forever. Someone who benefited from taking risks may continue pushing boundaries long after conditions change.

What worked once feels right again.

What hurts once feels dangerous forever.

Experience becomes a shortcut for decision-making, replacing careful evaluation with emotional memory.

Markets, careers, and opportunities constantly evolve.

Human memory does not adjust as quickly.

This mismatch creates problems.

People react to today's situations using yesterday's lessons—even when those lessons no longer apply. They prepare for crises that may never come, or chase opportunities that no longer exist.

The past becomes a filter through which all future choices are made.

Awareness changes everything.

When you recognize that your instincts are shaped by experience, you gain distance from them. You can ask better questions.

Am I reacting to the present, or replaying the past?

Is this fear justified, or is it familiar?

Is this confidence earned, or remembered?

These questions do not eliminate emotion.

They reduce its control.

None of this suggests that past experiences should be ignored.

They contain valuable lessons. They teach caution, resilience, and humility. But problems arise when experiences become rigid rules instead of flexible guides.

Experience should inform decisions—not dominate them.

A healthy relationship with money balances memory and reasoning.

It respects the past without being trapped by it. It learns from mistakes without turning them into permanent limitations. It allows growth while maintaining caution.

This balance is difficult.

But it is essential.

If there is one idea to carry forward from this chapter, it is this:

Your past explains your instincts, but it does not have to dictate your future.

Understanding this creates freedom—the freedom to update beliefs, adjust strategies, and respond to the present with clarity instead of fear.

Financial behavior is deeply shaped by past experiences.

Recognizing this influence allows you to make calmer, more intentional decisions.

Chapter 4: Why Rational Thinking Fails With Money

People like to believe they are rational with money.

They assume that when faced with a financial decision, they will carefully weigh options, analyze risks, and choose the most logical path. This belief feels reassuring. It suggests that good outcomes are simply the result of good thinking.

But money rarely operates in a rational environment.

It operates in the real world—where uncertainty, emotion, and incomplete information dominate.

Rational thinking works best in stable conditions.

If the rules are clear, the outcomes are predictable, and emotions are absent, logic performs well. But money decisions rarely meet these conditions. They are made under pressure, often with limited time and imperfect information.

The future is unknown.

Outcomes are delayed.

Consequences are uneven.

In such environments, rationality weakens.

Consider how people react during periods of uncertainty.

When prices rise quickly, logic says to be cautious. Emotion says to participate before the opportunity disappears. When prices fall sharply, logic says to evaluate long-term prospects. Emotion says to escape before things get worse.

Both reactions feel justified at the moment.

Fear and excitement create urgency. Urgency crowds out careful thinking. Decisions are made quickly, often based on stories and headlines rather than evidence.

This is not a flaw of intelligence.

It is a feature of human psychology.

Another reason rational thinking fails is delayed feedback.

Many financial decisions take years to reveal their true results. By the time outcomes appear, it is difficult to trace them back to specific choices. Success can be mistaken for skill. Failure can be blamed on bad luck.

Without clear feedback, people struggle to learn accurately.

They repeat behaviors that once worked—even if success was partly accidental. They avoid behaviors that once failed—even if failure was unavoidable.

Rational learning becomes distorted.

Confidence also interferes with rationality.

When people experience success, confidence grows. Confidence can be useful—it encourages action. But unchecked confidence often turns into overconfidence, leading people to underestimate risk and overestimate control.

Overconfidence is dangerous because it feels like rational certainty.

People believe they understand more than they do. They trust patterns that may not exist. They dismiss warnings that challenge their beliefs.

The result is not reckless behavior.

It is confident behavior that feels justified.

Social influence further weakens rational thinking.

People rarely make money decisions in isolation. They are influenced by friends, colleagues, media, and culture. When many people believe something, it begins to feel true.

Following the crowd reduces discomfort. Going against it requires emotional strength.

Rational thinking may point in one direction.

Social comfort pulls in another.

In moments of uncertainty, comfort often wins.

This does not mean rational thinking is useless.

It means rational thinking alone is insufficient.

Good financial behavior requires systems that account for human weakness. It requires strategies that reduce the need for constant decision-making. It requires rules that protect against emotional extremes.

The goal is not perfect rationality.

The goal is resilience.

The most successful financial plans assume that people will occasionally act irrationally. They are designed to survive mistakes, not avoid them entirely.

This is why simplicity often outperforms complexity. Simple plans are easier to follow under stress. Complex plans break when emotions rise.

If there is one lesson in this chapter, it is this:

The greatest financial risk is assuming you will always act rationally.

Accepting human limits is not pessimism.

It is practical wisdom.

Money decisions are made in emotional, uncertain environments.

Plans that acknowledge this reality are far more effective than those that assume perfect rationality.

Chapter 5: The Illusion of Control

People like to feel in control.

Control creates comfort. It gives the sense that outcomes are predictable and effort will be rewarded exactly as planned. In money, this feeling is especially attractive. If control is possible, then success feels earned and failure feels avoidable.

But much of what shapes financial outcomes lies outside personal control.

This gap between perceived control and reality quietly influences behavior—and often leads to costly mistakes.

The illusion of control appears when people confuse influence with certainty.

You can influence outcomes by saving, investing, working hard, and planning carefully. These actions matter. But influence is not the same as control. Markets fluctuate. Businesses fail. Careers change. Global events reshape economies.

Effort improves odds.

It does not guarantee results.

Yet when things go well, people often assume they are fully responsible. When things go poorly, they search for reasons they must have missed.

This asymmetry distorts judgment.

Success encourages confidence.

Confidence encourages risk.

When people experience positive outcomes, they often attribute them to skill rather than circumstance. This belief strengthens over time, especially during favorable conditions.

Opportunities seem obvious in hindsight. Decisions feel repeatable. Risk feels manageable.

But conditions change.

What once rewarded boldness may later punish it. What once felt safe may become fragile. The illusion of control delays recognition of this shift.

Failure reveals the illusion.

Unexpected losses feel shocking because they violate the belief that careful planning prevents bad outcomes. People ask, "How could this happen?" even when uncertainty was always present.

The problem was not lack of effort or intelligence.

It was a misplaced certainty.

Control was assumed where only probability existed.

This illusion also affects how people judge others.

Those who succeed are praised for insight. Those who fail are blamed for mistakes. The role of chance is minimized because it is uncomfortable to accept.

Acknowledging randomness challenges the idea that outcomes are fair and predictable. It introduces humility—and humility is harder to maintain than confidence.

Understanding the limits of control changes behavior.

It encourages margin of safety.

It encourages flexibility.

It encourages preparation for uncertainty rather than denial of it.

People who accept uncertainty build plans that can adapt. They avoid strategies that depend on perfect timing or flawless execution.

They prioritize survival over brilliance.

Letting go of the illusion of control does not mean giving up responsibility.

It means recognizing what can be managed—and what cannot.

You can control saving habits.

You can control spending choices.

You can control risk exposure.

You cannot control markets, timing, or unexpected events.

Wisdom lies in focusing energy where it matters.

If there is one idea to remember from this chapter, it is this:

Financial success comes from managing risk, not eliminating uncertainty.

When people stop trying to control everything, they start making decisions that last.

Believing you have more control than you do increases risk.

Accepting uncertainty leads to stronger, more resilient financial behavior.

Chapter 6: When Confidence Becomes Risk

Confidence is often praised as a strength.

In money, confidence encourages action. It helps people invest, start businesses, change careers, and commit to long-term plans. Without confidence, many opportunities would never be pursued.

But confidence has a quiet boundary.

Beyond that boundary, confidence turns into risk.

Confidence becomes dangerous when it stops questioning itself.

Early success can create the belief that good outcomes are the result of superior judgment. Decisions feel validated. Doubt fades. The need for caution seems unnecessary.

This is not arrogance.

It is reinforcement.

When behavior is rewarded, the mind assumes the behavior is correct. Over time, success feels repeatable—even when it was partly driven by favorable conditions.

The problem is that confidence grows faster than skill.

Skills develop slowly. They require feedback, reflection, and adjustment. Confidence, however, can expand rapidly after a few positive outcomes. This imbalance leads people to take on risks they do not fully understand.

The danger is not confidence itself.

The danger is untested confidence.

Financial environments often encourage this imbalance.

Periods of stability or growth make risk appear smaller than it is. When losses are rare, people forget they exist. When volatility is low, caution feels unnecessary.

Confidence feels rational because nothing seems to challenge it.

Until conditions change.

When confidence becomes a risk, warning signs appear.

People increase exposure without increasing safeguards.

They concentrate bets instead of diversifying.

They dismiss opposing views.

They interpret caution as weakness.

These behaviors feel logical within the confidence mindset.

But they reduce resilience.

The most damaging losses often occur not because people were reckless, but because they were certain.

Certainty removes flexibility. It narrows perspective. It discourages preparation for unfavorable outcomes.

When surprises occur, confident plans break more easily than cautious ones.

Healthy confidence looks different.

It acknowledges uncertainty.

It allows room for error.

It plans for outcomes beyond expectations.

Healthy confidence does not need to be loud. It does not demand constant proof. It is comfortable with humility.

This type of confidence builds systems rather than predictions.

The most successful financial decisions are often made by people who are confident enough to act, but humble enough to prepare for being wrong.

They assume they will make mistakes.

They design plans that survive them.

If there is one lesson in this chapter, it is this:

Confidence should support decisions, not replace caution.

Confidence opens doors.

Caution keeps them from closing suddenly.

Confidence is useful, but unchecked confidence increases risk.

The most durable financial strategies balance belief with humility.

Chapter 7: The Trap of Short-Term Thinking

Short-term thinking feels natural.

The human mind is wired to prioritize what is immediate, visible, and urgent. This instinct is useful for survival, but it becomes costly when applied to long-term financial decisions.

Money rewards patience.

Behavior resists it.

Short-term thinking focuses on recent events.

What happened last month feels more important than what might happen over the next decade. Recent success feels permanent. Recent losses feel predictive. This tendency leads people to overreact to temporary changes.

Markets fluctuate.

Careers move in cycles.

Businesses experience phases.

But short-term thinking treats every change as a signal rather than noise.

Urgency amplifies short-term behavior.

When people feel pressured—by news, peers, or expectations—they prioritize quick results. The desire for immediate improvement overrides long-term reasoning.

This is why people abandon sound strategies too early. Results do not appear fast enough. Discomfort arrives before rewards. The plan is questioned—not because it is flawed, but because it is slow.

Slow progress feels like failure in a world obsessed with speed.

Short-term thinking also distorts risk perception.

Immediate losses feel larger than future gains. People accept long-term costs to avoid short-term pain. They trade potential growth for temporary relief.

This trade rarely feels like a mistake at the moment. It feels like safety.

But over time, repeated short-term decisions compound into significant missed opportunities.

Long-term success often looks unimpressive in the short term.

Consistent saving does not create excitement. Steady investing rarely produces dramatic stories. Avoiding unnecessary risk rarely earns praise.

The most effective behaviors are often invisible.

This invisibility makes them difficult to commit to—especially when compared to flashy alternatives promising faster results.

Short-term thinking is reinforced by feedback.

Fast results provide quick validation. Slow strategies provide delayed reassurance. When feedback is delayed, doubt grows. People question whether patience is working, even when it is.

Without patience, consistency breaks.

Escaping short-term thinking requires shifting the goal.

Instead of asking, "Is this working right now?"

Ask, "Will this still make sense years from now?"

This shift reduces emotional reactions. It creates space for rational evaluation. It encourages decisions aligned with long-term values rather than temporary feelings.

If there is one idea to remember from this chapter, it is this:

Most financial mistakes are not the result of bad decisions, but of good decisions abandoned too early.

Patience is not passive.

It is an active choice to endure uncertainty in exchange for long-term stability.

Short-term thinking creates emotional reactions.

Long-term thinking creates durable results.

Chapter 8: Comparison Is the Most Expensive Habit

Comparison feels harmless.

It begins quietly—observing how others live, earn, spend, or invest. Over time, it shapes expectations. What once felt sufficient begins to feel inadequate. Progress is measured not by personal improvement, but by relative position.

This shift is subtle, yet powerful.

Comparison turns money into a moving target.

The problem with comparison is not awareness.

It is a misalignment.

People compare outcomes without comparing circumstances. They see success without seeing risk. They notice results without understanding timing, luck, or hidden costs.

What looks achievable may have required sacrifices that are unacceptable. What looks effortless may have been built on years of uncertainty.

Without context, comparison becomes distortion.

Comparison pressures behavior.

Spending increases to match perceived standards. Risk increases to accelerate progress. Decisions are made not because they align with personal goals, but because they reduce discomfort created by observing others.

This pressure rarely improves satisfaction.

It increases anxiety.

No matter how far someone advances, there will always be another comparison ahead.

Comparison also erodes patience.

When others appear to be moving faster, waiting feels like falling behind. Long-term plans are questioned. Conservative strategies feel insufficient. Shortcuts become tempting.

The focus shifts from building wealth to displaying progress.

This shift is costly.

One of the most overlooked aspects of comparison is visibility.

Modern life highlights results, not processes. Success is shared. Failure is hidden. Progress is curated. Risk is rarely discussed.

People compare their full reality to others' edited outcomes.

The comparison is unfair—but emotionally convincing.

True financial progress is personal.

It depends on values, goals, and comfort with risk. A strategy that works well for one person may create constant stress for another.

There is no universal pace.

There is no universal finish line.

Chasing someone else's version of success often leads away from one's own.

Breaking free from comparison requires redefining success.

Success is not outpacing others.

It is reducing dependence on external validation.

When financial decisions are guided by personal priorities rather than social pressure, satisfaction increases—even if progress appears slower.

Peace is often quieter than achievement.

If there is one lesson in this chapter, it is this:

Comparison turns financial decisions into emotional reactions rather than intentional choices.

Wealth grows when focus turns inward.

Comparison increases spending, risk, and dissatisfaction.

Alignment with personal goals leads to calmer, more sustainable progress.

Chapter 9: Time Is the Only Advantage Everyone Gets

Most advantages in life are unevenly distributed.

Some people start with more resources, better connections, or earlier opportunities. Others face constraints that limit choices from the beginning. These differences shape outcomes in powerful ways.

Time is the exception.

Everyone moves through it at the same pace.

Time is often misunderstood in money.

People focus on timing—trying to choose the perfect moment to act. They wait for clarity, certainty, or ideal conditions. When those conditions do not appear, hesitation follows.

But timing is unpredictable.

Time, used consistently, is reliable.

The greatest financial advantage is not acting at the perfect moment. It is staying involved long enough for small decisions to grow.

Time magnifies behavior.

Good habits become powerful when repeated over years. Bad habits become costly when left unchecked. The effect is gradual and often invisible in the beginning.

This invisibility causes doubt.

People underestimate slow progress because they cannot see it happening. They overestimate sudden change because it feels dramatic.

Time rewards consistency, not intensity.

One of the most important roles of time is recovery.

Mistakes happen. Setbacks occur. Losses are unavoidable. Time allows errors to fade in importance—as long as survival is maintained.

Without time, there is no second chance.

This is why avoiding permanent damage matters more than maximizing short-term gains. Time cannot help if the process ends too early.

Time also reduces the pressure to be right.

When decisions are spread over long periods, individual mistakes matter less. The need for perfect judgment disappears. Progress becomes the result of endurance rather than precision.

This shift changes behavior.

People become calmer.

They tolerate volatility better.

They remain consistent through uncertainty.

Impatience works against time.

The desire for quick results shortens horizons. Short horizons increase sensitivity to noise. Noise creates emotional reactions. Emotional reactions disrupt consistency.

The cycle breaks when time is respected as an ally rather than a constraint.

Using time effectively requires a mindset shift.

Instead of asking, "What will work fastest?"

Ask, "What will still make sense years from now?"

This question filters out fragile strategies. It favors durability over excitement. It aligns decisions with long-term stability.

If there is one idea to remember from this chapter, it is this:

Time does the heavy lifting when behavior stays consistent.

No intelligence advantage is as powerful as patience combined with survival.

Time rewards consistency and resilience.

Those who stay in the game long enough allow small advantages to grow into meaningful outcomes.

Chapter 10: Luck, Skill, and Timing

People prefer clear explanations for success.

Skill feels earned. It fits the idea that effort leads to reward. Luck, on the other hand, feels uncomfortable. It suggests outcomes are partly random, unpredictable, and unfair.

So when success appears, skill is celebrated.

When failure appears, mistakes are analyzed.

Luck quietly disappears from the story.

In reality, most outcomes are a combination of all three: skill, luck, and timing.

Skill improves the quality of decisions.

Timing influences when opportunities appear.

Luck determines how external factors align.

Ignoring any one of these creates an incomplete picture.

Skill matters, but it operates within boundaries.

Well-prepared people increase their chances of success. They recognize opportunities earlier. They respond better to challenges. Over long periods, skill raises the probability of favorable outcomes.

But probability is not certainty.

Even the most skilled individuals face outcomes shaped by factors they could not control. External conditions, unexpected events, and randomness influence results in ways that planning cannot eliminate.

Timing often determines whether skill is rewarded.

The same decision made at different moments can produce opposite results. Conditions matter. Environments change. What works during one period may fail in another.

Timing is rarely obvious in advance.

It is often recognized only in hindsight—after outcomes are known.

Luck plays a larger role than most people admit.

Luck affects opportunities encountered, connections formed, and obstacles avoided. It influences which risks succeed and which fail.

This does not mean effort is irrelevant.

It means effort operates alongside randomness.

Recognizing luck does not diminish achievement.

It introduces humility.

Humility improves decision-making.

When people accept the role of luck, they become less judgmental of others and less overconfident in themselves. They prepare for uncertainty. They avoid strategies that rely on perfect outcomes.

They build margins of safety.

Misunderstanding luck leads to dangerous conclusions.

Success is assumed to be fully repeatable. Failure is assumed to be fully preventable. Both beliefs encourage excessive risk-taking and unrealistic expectations.

Reality is more nuanced.

Skill improves odds.

Luck determines results.

Time reveals patterns.

The most sustainable financial behavior respects all three.

It develops skill without assuming mastery.

It acknowledges timing without trying to predict it.

It accepts luck without depending on it.

This balance creates resilience.

If there is one idea to remember from this chapter, it is this:

Respecting luck keeps confidence grounded and expectations realistic.

Wealth grows best when humility guides behavior.

Skill matters, but outcomes are influenced by timing and luck.

Acknowledging this leads to wiser, more durable financial decisions.

Chapter 11: Why Survival Matters More Than Growth

Growth is celebrated.

It represents progress, success, and forward movement. In money, growth is often treated as the ultimate goal. Faster growth is admired. Bigger returns are praised. More aggressive strategies attract attention.

But growth has a silent prerequisite.

You must survive long enough to experience it.

Many financial failures are not caused by bad ideas.

They are caused by good ideas taken too far.

People pursue growth without considering fragility. They accept risks that cannot be recovered from. When conditions change, their strategies collapse—not because they were foolish, but because they left no room for error.

Survival is rarely exciting.

But it is essential.

Survival means avoiding irreversible damage.

Temporary losses can be recovered. Permanent losses cannot. Once a strategy ends, time no longer works in your favor.

This is why the first rule of long-term financial behavior is simple:

Stay in the game.

Survival requires restraint.

It means not using all available resources. It means avoiding strategies that depend on perfect outcomes. It means accepting slower progress in exchange for durability.

This restraint often feels unnecessary during good times.

When things are going well, caution feels excessive. Safety looks inefficient. Risk seems manageable.

Until it isn't.

Growth-focused thinking often underestimates uncertainty.

It assumes favorable conditions will continue. It assumes past success predicts future outcomes. It assumes risks are visible and manageable.

These assumptions work—until they don't.

Survival-focused thinking makes fewer assumptions. It prepares for unfavorable scenarios even when they seem unlikely.

Survival also protects decision-making.

When resources are stretched thin, pressure increases. Pressure leads to emotional decisions. Emotional decisions increase risk.

By maintaining buffers—financial, emotional, and psychological—people preserve clarity.

Clarity supports consistency.

Long-term success favors those who endure.

Many strategies work for a while. Very few work forever. The difference between lasting success and temporary success is not intelligence—it is sustainability.

Survivors benefit from time.

Non-survivors do not.

Choosing survival over growth does not mean avoiding ambition.

It means sequencing goals.

First, build stability.

Then, pursue growth within safe limits.

This approach may appear slower, but it dramatically increases the odds of reaching meaningful outcomes.

If there is one lesson in this chapter, it is this:

The most important financial skill is avoiding decisions that remove you from the game.

Growth is optional.

Survival is mandatory.

Long-term wealth depends more on avoiding permanent loss than on maximizing short-term growth.

Survival allows time and consistency to do their work.

Chapter 12: Risk Looks Different to Different People

Risk is often spoken about as if it were objective.

Percentages, probabilities, and projections create the impression that risk can be measured precisely and understood universally. But risk is not experienced through numbers alone.

It is felt.

And what people feel about risk depends heavily on their circumstances.

Two people can face the same financial decision and perceive completely different levels of danger.

For one person, a loss might mean discomfort.

For another, it might mean instability.

These differences shape behavior more than statistics ever could.

Risk is personal.

Income stability, savings, responsibilities, and emotional tolerance all influence how much uncertainty someone can accept. What feels manageable to one person may feel overwhelming to another.

Neither perspective is wrong.

They reflect different realities.

This is why uniform advice about risk often fails.

Telling everyone to take more risks ignores individual consequences. Telling everyone to be conservative ignores opportunity costs.

Good financial behavior aligns risk with capacity—not with averages.

Risk tolerance is not static.

It changes over time. Life events, experiences, and responsibilities reshape comfort levels. A strategy that once felt reasonable may later feel stressful. Adjusting is not failure.

It is an adaptation.

Ignoring personal risk tolerance leads to fragile plans.

When people follow strategies that make them uncomfortable, consistency breaks. Fear rises during uncertainty. Decisions are reversed at the worst moments.

A plan that cannot be followed under stress is not a good plan—no matter how impressive it looks on paper.

The goal is not to eliminate risk.

It is to choose risks that allow endurance.

Endurance requires psychological comfort as much as financial capacity. When risk aligns with temperament, patience becomes easier. When it does not, emotion takes control.

Understanding personal risk creates freedom.

It allows people to design strategies they can live with—not just admire. It removes guilt from cautious behavior and overconfidence from aggressive behavior.

Balance replaces pressure.

If there is one idea to remember from this chapter, it is this:

The right amount of risk is the amount you can live with through uncertainty.

The risk of forcing abandonment is too much.

Risk is subjective and personal.

Aligning risk with individual capacity leads to calmer, more sustainable financial decisions.

Chapter 13: The Difference Between Looking Rich and Being Wealthy

Looking rich is visible.

Being wealthy is quiet.

This difference shapes more financial outcomes than most people realize.

Looking rich is about appearance.

It shows up in possessions, lifestyles, and public signals of success. It is designed to be noticed. It communicates progress, status, and achievement—often in real time.

Being wealthy is different.

It is built through what is not seen: savings, flexibility, patience, and the ability to say no. Wealth rarely announces itself. It exists in margins, options, and resilience.

The confusion between the two is costly.

When people focus on looking rich, spending rises to match expectations. Income increases are quickly absorbed by lifestyle upgrades. Financial progress becomes fragile because it depends on continuous performance.

Being wealthy, on the other hand, depends on accumulation—not display.

Accumulation is slower.

It is less exciting.

It attracts less attention.

But it compounds.

The pressure to look successful often comes from comparison.

When others appear to be advancing, maintaining appearances feels necessary. This pressure encourages spending decisions that prioritize perception over security.

Over time, appearance replaces purpose.

Wealth is not defined by what you own.

It is defined by what you can control.

Control over time.

Control over choices.

Control over uncertainty.

These forms of control are rarely visible. They do not photograph well. They do not impress quickly.

But they provide stability.

One of the most powerful benefits of wealth is optionality.

Optionality is the ability to choose.

To walk away from bad situations.

To wait for better opportunities.

To absorb setbacks without panic.

This freedom comes from resources that are not immediately consumed.

Looking rich consumes resources.

Being wealthy preserves them.

This trade-off explains why many people who appear successful feel stressed, while others who live modestly feel secure. Appearance creates expectations. Wealth creates independence.

Choosing wealth over appearance requires restraint.

It means resisting social pressure. It means accepting slower visible progress. It means prioritizing future flexibility over present validation.

This choice is rarely celebrated.

But it is deeply rewarding.

If there is one idea to remember from this chapter, it is this:

True wealth is the ability to live on your own terms, not the ability to display success.

The quiet side of wealth is where freedom lives.

Looking rich focuses on consumption and perception.

Being wealthy focuses on control, flexibility, and long-term stability.

Chapter 14: Why More Rarely Feels Enough

Progress should create satisfaction.

Yet in money, progress often creates new dissatisfaction.

As income grows, expectations rise. As resources increase, desires expand. What once felt like success becomes the new baseline.

This cycle is not accidental.

It is human nature.

The feeling of "enough" is fragile.

It is influenced by surroundings, comparisons, and changing goals. When people improve their circumstances, their reference point shifts. Comfort becomes normal. Normal becomes insufficient.

More becomes the expectation.

This is why financial goals keep moving.

The target is reached, but fulfillment is temporary. New benchmarks appear. The pursuit continues—not because needs remain unmet, but because expectations have changed.

The problem is not ambition.

It is adaptation without reflection.

More rarely feels enough because satisfaction is relative.

People measure progress against peers, past experiences, and imagined futures. These comparisons distort perception. Gains feel smaller when surrounded by larger gains elsewhere.

This relative evaluation fuels continuous striving.

Chasing more also increases pressure.

Higher standards require higher performance. Fixed costs rise. Flexibility decreases. The margin for error narrows.

More success brings more dependency.

What was meant to create freedom begins to reduce it.

Enough is not a number.

It is a decision.

It is the point at which additional gain no longer improves well-being. This point differs for everyone. It depends on values, lifestyle preferences, and tolerance for risk.

Recognizing enough creates stability.

Defining enough does not mean stopping progress.

It means choosing progress intentionally.

When people know what is enough, they can pursue growth without being controlled by it. They can enjoy success without becoming dependent on constant expansion.

The absence of "enough" creates endless motion.

The presence of "enough" creates calm.

Calm improves decision-making. Calm supports patience. Calm protects long-term goals.

If there is one idea to remember from this chapter, it is this:

Without a clear definition of enough, progress never feels satisfying.

Wealth without contentment becomes another form of pressure.

More does not automatically create happiness or security.

Defining "enough" brings clarity, balance, and long-term peace.

Chapter 15: The Power of Having "Enough"

Enough is a powerful idea.

Not because it limits ambition, but because it creates direction. When people know what enough looks like, decisions become clearer. Trade-offs become easier. Progress feels intentional rather than endless.

Enough transforms money from a chase into a tool.

Without enough, every gain invites another demand.

With enough, gains become optional.

This distinction changes behavior in subtle but meaningful ways. People with a clear sense of enough take fewer unnecessary risks. They resist social pressure more easily. They protect what they have built.

Enough creates boundaries.

The power of enough is not in restriction.

It is freedom.

When people reach a point where their needs, comfort, and security are met, additional money stops controlling decisions. Time, health, relationships, and peace regain importance.

Money becomes supportive rather than dominant.

Enough also reduces fear.

When people know they have sufficient resources, uncertainty feels manageable. Setbacks feel temporary. Decisions are made with patience rather than urgency.

Fear thrives in scarcity.

Calm thrives in sufficiency.

Many financial regrets come from ignoring enough.

People push beyond comfort to reach higher targets. They accept stress in exchange for growth. They sacrifice flexibility for scale.

Often, they later realize that the trade-off was unnecessary.

Enough was already there.

Having enough does not mean settling.

It means choosing growth with awareness.

People can still pursue goals, build wealth, and seek improvement. The difference is motivation. Growth becomes a choice, not a requirement for self-worth or security.

This distinction prevents burnout.

Enough also protects long-term plans.

When people are not desperate for more, they can wait. They can tolerate slow progress. They can endure volatility without abandoning strategies.

Enough supports consistency.

If there is one idea to remember from this chapter, it is this:

Knowing when you have enough is one of the most important financial skills.

It creates peace without stopping progress.

Enough provides clarity and freedom.

Defining it allows wealth to support life instead of controlling it.

Chapter 16: Freedom Is the Real Return on Money

Money is often measured in numbers.

Balances, returns, percentages, and milestones dominate how success is evaluated. These metrics are useful, but they miss the deeper purpose money serves in life.

The true return on money is freedom.

Freedom is the ability to choose.

To decide how time is spent.

To walk away from unhealthy situations.

To respond to change without panic.

These choices are rarely available to people who are financially stretched—even if their income appears high.

Many people confuse income with freedom.

Income provides cash flow. Freedom requires margin.

Margin is the space between what you have and what you need. It allows flexibility. It absorbs uncertainty. It reduces dependence on constant performance.

Without margin, income becomes fragile.

Freedom grows quietly.

It is built through savings, patience, and restraint. It increases when obligations are manageable and expectations are controlled. It disappears when commitments outpace resources.

Freedom does not demand visibility.

It demands sustainability.

This is why some high earners feel trapped.

Their lifestyle requires constant income. Their choices are limited by obligations. Their margin is thin.

They appear successful.

They lack flexibility.

Freedom-oriented thinking changes priorities.

Instead of maximizing returns, it focuses on minimizing dependence. Instead of chasing the highest growth, it values reliability. Instead of optimizing for appearance, it optimizes for control.

These shifts reduce stress.

Money used for freedom is rarely flashy.

It sits quietly. It waits patiently. It provides options when needed. It protects against unwanted pressure.

Its value is realized during difficult moments—not during celebration.

Freedom also supports long-term thinking.

When basic security is assured, people can plan further ahead. They can tolerate uncertainty. They can make decisions based on values rather than urgency.

Freedom improves judgment.

If there is one idea to remember from this chapter, it is this:

Money's greatest return is the ability to live with choice rather than constraint.

Wealth is meaningful when it expands life—not when it complicates it.

True financial success is measured by freedom and flexibility.

Money that creates choice is more valuable than money that creates status.

Chapter 17: Patience Beats Intelligence

Intelligence is admired.

It signals capability, understanding, and problem-solving ability. In money, intelligence is often assumed to be the primary driver of success. Smarter decisions should lead to better outcomes.

Yet over long periods, patience often matters more.

Patience allows time to work.

Intelligent strategies require time to reveal their benefits. Without patience, even the best ideas fail to deliver results. People abandon plans not because they are flawed, but because they take longer than expected.

The gap between action and reward tests discipline.

Impatience creates unnecessary movement.

When progress feels slow, people change direction. They switch strategies, chase trends, or react to short-term noise. Each change resets progress.

Consistency breaks.

Momentum disappears.

Patience also reduces errors.

Quick decisions often amplify emotion. Slow decisions allow reflection. Patience creates space between stimulus and response.

This space improves judgment.

Intelligence without patience leads to over-optimization.

People seek perfect strategies, ideal timing, and optimal outcomes. They analyze endlessly or adjust constantly. The result is complexity without durability.

Patience simplifies behavior.

Long-term success favors those who can wait.

They tolerate uncertainty.

They endure volatility.

They allow compounding to operate.

These qualities are not measured by intelligence tests.

Patience is not passive.

It is active restraint.

It requires resisting impulses, ignoring distractions, and trusting processes that unfold gradually. This restraint is difficult in environments that reward speed and visibility.

Yet it is essential.

The most successful financial outcomes often look boring.

They lack dramatic stories. They lack frequent action. They rely on time rather than cleverness.

Boring behavior compounded over years beats brilliant behavior abandoned early.

If there is one idea to remember from this chapter, it is this:

Intelligence may start the journey, but patience determines how far it goes.

Wealth grows when behavior stays consistent long enough.

Patience allows time and consistency to create results.

Without patience, intelligence is often wasted.

Chapter 18: Simple Rules Work Best

Complexity feels sophisticated.

Detailed strategies, advanced tools, and layered systems create the impression of control and intelligence. In money, complexity often appears safer because it seems thorough.

But complexity breaks under stress.

Simple rules endure.

They are easier to remember, easier to follow, and easier to maintain when emotions rise. During uncertainty, simplicity provides clarity. It reduces the number of decisions required when judgment is most vulnerable.

Simplicity supports consistency.

Complex systems demand precision.

They assume ideal behavior, perfect timing, and constant attention. When one element fails, the entire system weakens. Under pressure, mistakes multiply.

Simple rules allow errors.

They are forgiving. They survive imperfection.

Most financial mistakes do not come from lack of information.

They come from overreaction.

Simple rules limit reaction. They create boundaries that protect against emotional decisions. When rules are clear, behavior becomes automatic.

Automatic behavior is stable behavior.

Examples of simple rules are not impressive.

They do not optimize every outcome. They do not guarantee maximum returns. They trade perfection for durability.

This trade-off is intentional.

Simple rules also reduce regret.

When decisions are guided by clear principles rather than constant evaluation, outcomes feel acceptable—even when they are not ideal. The process is trusted.

Trust reduces stress.

The most effective financial plans are often built on a few core ideas repeated consistently.

Not constant adjustments.

Not frequent innovation.

Not endless optimization.

Consistency outperforms creativity over time.

If there is one idea to remember from this chapter, it is this:

Simple rules are not limiting; they are stabilizing.

They allow long-term behavior to remain intact.

Simplicity improves consistency and resilience.

Simple rules outperform complex strategies under real-world conditions.

Chapter 19: Boring Strategies Win

Boring rarely gets attention.

In money, excitement is celebrated. Fast gains, bold moves, and dramatic stories dominate conversation. Boring approaches are dismissed as outdated, slow, or uninspiring.

Yet boring strategies quietly outperform.

Boring strategies work because they are repeatable.

They do not rely on rare events or perfect timing. They are designed to function across different conditions. Their success comes from consistency, not brilliance.

Consistency compounds.

Exciting strategies demand constant engagement.

They require frequent decisions, emotional involvement, and precise execution. When conditions change, stress increases. Mistakes become more likely.

Boring strategies reduce involvement.

They allow distance from daily noise. They create space for long-term thinking. They minimize emotional interference.

Boring strategies also align with human behavior.

People are more likely to stick with plans that do not demand constant attention. Low-maintenance approaches survive busy periods, distractions, and uncertainty.

Survival favors boredom.

The appeal of excitement often comes from visibility.

Dramatic outcomes are easier to notice and share. Quiet progress is rarely discussed. This creates a distorted perception of success.

What is visible is not always sustainable.

Boring strategies protect against overconfidence.

They discourage frequent action. They reduce the temptation to react. They assume average outcomes rather than exceptional ones.

This assumption improves durability.

Long-term success often belongs to those who avoid drama.

They resist trends.

They ignore noise.

They focus on steady behavior.

Their progress appears slow—until it is not.

If there is one idea to remember from this chapter, it is this:

What feels boring today often looks brilliant in hindsight.

Boring strategies win because they survive.

Boring approaches support consistency and endurance.

Quiet progress outperforms exciting behavior over long periods.

Chapter 20: The Value of Optionality

Optionality is rarely discussed.

It does not show up in performance charts or success stories. It does not create immediate rewards. Yet it quietly shapes the quality of financial lives.

Optionality is the ability to choose.

Choice is powerful because the future is uncertain.

When conditions change, those with options can adapt. They can wait, adjust, or change direction. Those without options are forced to react.

Forced decisions are rarely optimal.

Optionality is created through flexibility.

Low fixed costs.

Manageable obligations.

Accessible resources.

These factors allow movement. They reduce dependence on specific outcomes. They create resilience.

Many people trade optionality for short-term gains.

They commit fully to single paths. They maximize leverage. They eliminate buffers. These decisions can accelerate progress—but they also increase fragility.

When circumstances change, options disappear.

Optionality does not require perfection.

It requires margin.

Margin allows patience. It allows experimentation. It allows mistakes without catastrophic consequences.

Margin is not wasted potential.

It is insurance against uncertainty.

Optionality also improves decision-making.

When people are not pressured by necessity, they think more clearly. They can evaluate opportunities without urgency. They can decline paths that do not align with long-term goals.

Freedom of choice enhances judgment.

Optionality is often invisible.

It exists in what you do not spend, what you do not commit, and what you keep available. Its benefits appear during difficult moments—not during good times.

Those who value optionality plan for change rather than certainty.

If there is one idea to remember from this chapter, it is this:

Optionality is not about predicting the future; it is about being prepared for many futures.

Wealth grows stronger when choices remain open.

Optionality provides flexibility and resilience.

Having choices matters more than maximizing any single outcome.

Chapter 21: Money and Happiness

Money is often linked to happiness.

It promises comfort, security, and opportunity. It reduces certain stresses and expands choices. In many ways, money does improve quality of life.

But its influence has limits.

Money is most powerful at reducing pain.

It helps meet basic needs. It removes constant worry. It provides stability. These effects are meaningful and often underestimated.

Beyond this point, money's impact changes.

More does not remove all dissatisfaction. It does not eliminate uncertainty. It does not guarantee peace.

Happiness is shaped by more than financial security.

Health, relationships, purpose, and autonomy play significant roles. Money can support these areas—but it cannot replace them.

When money becomes the sole focus, imbalance grows.

Many people expect money to deliver emotional fulfillment.

They assume higher income or greater wealth will solve dissatisfaction. When this expectation is unmet, disappointment follows.

The problem is not money.

It is a misplaced expectation.

Money contributes to happiness when it supports life rather than competes with it.

When it creates time instead of consuming it.

When it reduces stress instead of increasing it.

When it aligns with values instead of conflicting with them.

In these cases, money becomes a quiet enhancer.

The pursuit of happiness through money alone often backfires.

It encourages endless comparison. It fuels dissatisfaction. It increases pressure to maintain progress.

Happiness becomes conditional.

A healthier relationship with money recognizes its role.

Money is a tool, not a destination.

It can improve circumstances. It can increase freedom. But happiness depends on how money is used—not how much is accumulated.

If there is one idea to remember from this chapter, it is this:

Money supports happiness best when it is used to reduce stress and increase freedom, not to chase fulfillment.

Wealth that aligns with life creates balance.

Money improves happiness up to a point.

Beyond that, its value depends on how it supports well-being and freedom.

Chapter 22: A Long-Term Way to Think About Wealth

Wealth is often framed as an outcome.

A number to reach.

A level to achieve.

A finish line to cross.

But lasting wealth is not an event.

It is a way of thinking.

A long-term perspective changes everything.

It shifts focus from short-term results to durable behavior. It replaces urgency with patience. It values consistency over intensity.

In this perspective, progress is measured by stability, not speed.

Long-term thinking accepts uncertainty.

It recognizes that the future cannot be predicted with precision. Instead of seeking certainty, it prepares for variability. It builds systems that can adapt rather than strategies that depend on perfect conditions.

Adaptability outlasts precision.

This mindset also values humility.

It acknowledges the role of luck. It avoids overconfidence. It remains open to learning. Humility keeps behavior flexible when circumstances change.

Rigid thinking breaks.

Flexible thinking survives.

A long-term approach prioritizes survival and optionality.

It avoids irreversible decisions. It maintains margins. It protects the ability to choose. These qualities ensure that time remains an ally.

Time rewards those who endure.

Wealth built this way often looks unimpressive at first.

It grows quietly. It compounds steadily. It avoids drama. Over time, its strength becomes undeniable—not through visibility, but through resilience.

A long-term way to think about wealth is not about doing more.

It is about doing fewer things well—and repeating them patiently.

If there is one final idea to carry forward from this book, it is this:

Wealth is not about winning quickly. It is about staying consistent long enough for small advantages to become meaningful.

The quiet side of wealth is built slowly—but it lasts.

True wealth is a combination of patience, resilience, and self-awareness.

When behavior aligns with long-term thinking, money becomes a source of stability rather than stress.

About the Author

G.P. Upadhyay writes about money, behavior, and long-term thinking.

His work focuses on the human side of financial decisions—how emotions, habits, and patience shape outcomes more than intelligence or complexity. He believes that sustainable wealth is built quietly through awareness, consistency, and restraint.

When not writing, he studies patterns in decision-making, explores systems that support long-term stability, and works on projects that emphasize clarity over noise.

www.ingramcontent.com/pod-product-compliance
Lightning Source LLC
LaVergne TN
LVHW022316200926
848481LV00004B/1362
* 9 7 9 8 2 3 3 0 4 6 6 0 5 *